PRIMARY SOURCES OF AMERICAN WARS™

The American Revolutionary War

Georgene Poulakidas

The Rosen Publishing Group's
PowerKids Press™
PRIMARY SOURCE

For my cousin, Dena, and her husband, Christos

Published in 2006 by The Rosen Publishing Group, Inc.
29 East 21st Street, New York, NY 10010

First Edition

Editor: Eric Fein
Book Design: Erica Clendening
Photo Researcher: Peter Tomlinson

Photo Credits: Cover, pp. 4, 12, 14 © Bettmann / Corbis; pp. 4 (inset), 6 (inset) Library of Congress, Manuscript Division; pp. 6, 10 (inset) Hulton Archive / Getty Images; pp. 8, 14 (inset), 20 Library of Congress, Prints and Photographs Division; p. 8 (inset) Library of Congress, Rare Book and Special Collections Division; p. 10 Print Collection, Miriam and Ira D. Wallach Division of Art, Prints, and Photographs, New York Public Library Astor, Lenox, and Tilden Foundations; p. 12 (inset) Library of Congress, Geography and Map Division; pp. 16, 18 Architect of the Capitol; p. 16 (inset) Independence National Historical Park; p. 18 (inset) © Corbis; p. 20 (inset) National Archives and Records Administration.

Library of Congress Cataloging-in-Publication Data

Poulakidas, Georgene.
    The American Revolutionary War / Georgene Poulakidas.— 1st ed.
    p. cm. — (Primary sources of American wars)
    Includes bibliographical references (p.) and index.
    Contents: England's colonies in North America — Paying the cost of war — Trouble in
Boston—The Revolution begins—Fighting for independence—The Battles of Trenton
and Princeton — The Battle of Saratoga — End of the war — The new nation.
    ISBN 1-4042-2680-X (lib. bdg.)
    1. United States—History—Revolution, 1775–1783—Juvenile literature. [1. United
States—History—Revolution, 1775–1783.] I. Title. II. Series.

    E208.P68 2006
    973.3—dc22

                                                                    2003021081

Manufactured in the United States of America

Contents

The Capitall Lawes of New-England; as they stand
now in force in the Common-Wealth.

BY THE COVRT,

In the Years 1641. 1642.

Capitall Lawes, Established within the Iurisdiction of Massachusets.

This page is from a collection of colonists' laws called The General Laws and Liberties of the Massachusets Colony. *This collection was printed in 1672.*

England's Colonies in North America

Between 1607 and 1733, England established 13 colonies in North America. Many colonists earned their living as farmers. Other colonists, especially those in the northern colonies, such as Massachusetts, made their living from fishing, whaling, and shipbuilding. Some colonists made their living by trading goods with England and other nations.

The people who came to the colonies from Europe wanted a better way of life. In America, they set up local governments that created laws meant to keep the colonies operating well. However, England had control over some of the laws the colonies passed, including those laws having to do with trade.

■ *Whaling was an important business for many people who lived in the northern colonies. Men sailed in ships, hunting for whales. When a whale was spotted, men attacked with spearlike weapons called harpoons.*

(279)

Anno quinto

Georgii III. Regis.

C A P. XII.

An Act for granting and applying certain Stamp Duties, and other Duties, in the British Colonies and Plantations in America, towards further defraying the Expences of defending, protecting, and securing the same; and for amending such Parts of the several Acts of Parliament relating to the Trade and Revenues of the said Colonies and Plantations, as direct the Manner of determining and recovering the Penalties and Forfeitures therein mentioned.

WHEREAS by an Act made in the last Session of Parliament, several Duties were granted, continued, and appropriated, towards defraying the Expences of defending, protecting, and securing, the British Colonies and Plantations in America: And whereas it is just and necessary, that Provision be made for raising a further Revenue within Your Majesty's Dominions in America, towards defraying the said Expences: We, Your Majesty's most dutiful and loyal Subjects, the Commons of Great Britain in Parliament assembled, have

■ *The Stamp Act (left) taxed colonists for stamps they used on official papers. It was one of the first taxes placed on the colonies. It created much anger within the colonies toward England.*

6

Paying the Cost of War

From 1754 to 1763, England and its American colonies fought side by side in the French and Indian War. The war was fought against France and its Native American **allies** in the colonies and in Canada. England and its colonies won the war, allowing England to gain control of Canada. England wanted the colonies to help pay the costs of the war because the war had been fought to protect the colonies. To raise money, England passed laws, called acts, that placed high taxes on the goods colonists needed, such as sugar, paper, and tea. Many of these goods came from England or its other colonies. The American colonists thought that England was being unfair and refused to agree to England's laws.

■ *This painting shows British general Edward Braddock and his soldiers fighting Native Americans during the French and Indian War. The British were on their way to attack Fort Duquesne, now known as Pittsburgh, Pennsylvania.*

■ *During the Boston Tea Party (above), colonists dumped over 300 boxes of tea into Boston Harbor.*

Trouble in Boston

Many colonists formed groups to **protest** England's unfair taxes and laws. The most active of these groups was the Sons of Liberty. This group was located in Boston, Massachusetts. It was led by Samuel Adams and John Hancock.

In March 1770, a crowd of angry colonists got into a fight with British soldiers. The soldiers opened fire, killing five colonists. This event was called the **Boston Massacre**.

In 1773, a group of colonists threw a **shipload** of tea into Boston Harbor. They did this to protest a tax on tea. Their actions became known as the Boston Tea Party. It caused England to create laws to punish the colonists. The colonists called these laws the **Intolerable Acts**.

■ *In 1770, Paul Revere made this picture (left) of the Boston Massacre. Revere would later play an important role in the American Revolutionary War. In 1775, he rode to warn American colonists of an attack the British planned on the towns of Lexington and Concord.*

■ England's King George Ⅲ issued these orders (left) for the arrest of the colonial leaders who were causing unrest.

10

The Revolution Begins

In September 1774, colonial leaders met in Philadelphia, Pennsylvania. They formed the **First Continental Congress**. Their purpose was to unite the colonies to take action against England.

In April 1775, British general Thomas Gage was ordered to arrest the colonial leaders causing unrest in Boston. However, the leaders learned of the British plans and escaped. Gage then sent soldiers to capture a supply of the colonists' **weapons** in nearby Concord. The battle that followed marked the beginning of the **American Revolutionary War**. On April 19, 1775, the first battle took place in Lexington, which is about 11 miles (17.7 km) from Boston. The local American soldiers, called **minutemen**, were able to hold off the British. The fighting continued 6 miles (9.6 km) away in Concord. The colonists' fighting spirit forced the British troops to withdraw to Boston.

■ *This picture of the Battle of Lexington was made by Amos Doolittle. Doolittle went to the battlefield after the fighting had ended. He talked to people who had watched the battle and used their accounts to create the picture.*

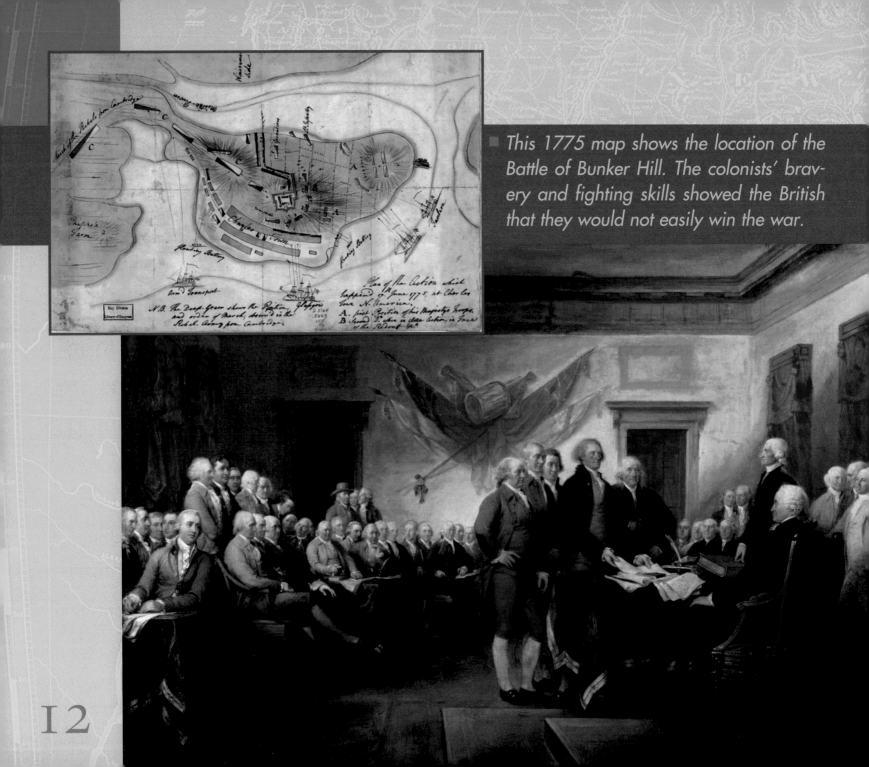

This 1775 map shows the location of the Battle of Bunker Hill. The colonists' bravery and fighting skills showed the British that they would not easily win the war.

Fighting for Independence

During the spring of 1775, the Second Continental Congress met in Philadelphia. At the meeting, the congress established the **Continental army**. George Washington was made its leader. Although outnumbered by the British army, the colonists now had a single army to fight the war. On June 17, 1775, the Battle of Bunker Hill was fought in Boston. Although the British won the battle, about 1,000 British soldiers were killed or hurt.

In June 1776, the congress asked Thomas Jefferson and four other colonial leaders to write a document that would explain the colonists' fight for freedom to the world. On July 4, 1776, the Continental Congress approved this document. It was called the **Declaration of Independence**.

■ *The signing of the Declaration of Independence (left) was a very important moment in the history of the United States. This painting by John Trumbull shows colonial leaders at the signing of the document.*

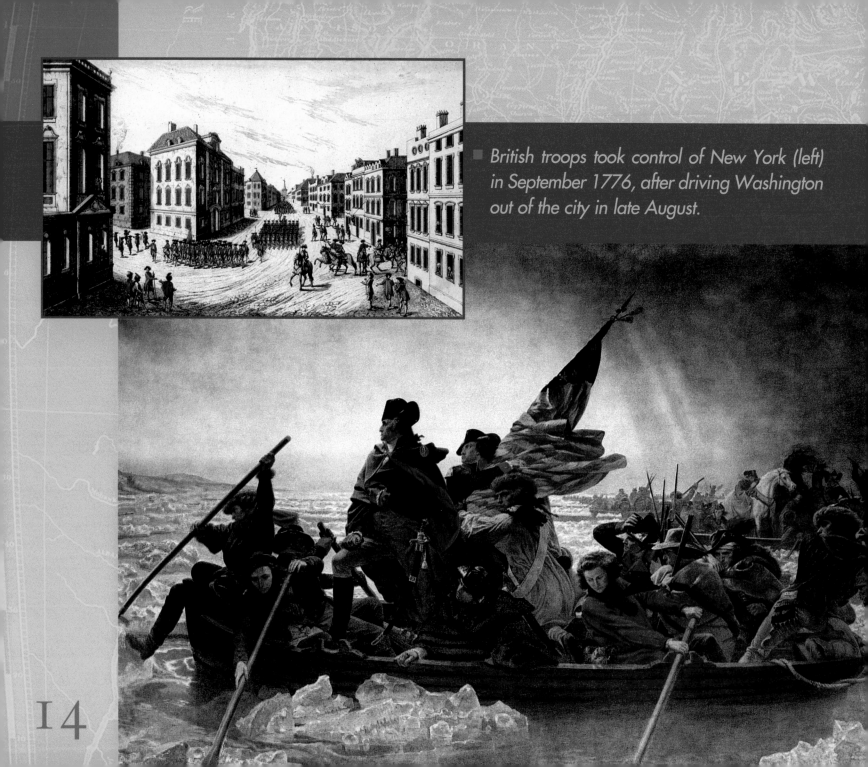

British troops took control of New York (left) in September 1776, after driving Washington out of the city in late August.

The Battles of Trenton and Princeton

In September 1776, the British took control of New York. Washington moved his troops from the New York area to New Jersey, and then to Pennsylvania. From there, he would attack the British forces who were occupying Trenton, New Jersey, across the Delaware River.

On December 26, 1776, Washington led about 2,400 troops across the Delaware River. They marched through the cold night, attacking the enemy the next morning. Within a few hours, they captured over 900 British prisoners. On January 3, 1777, Washington and his troops fought and defeated enemy forces in the Battle of Princeton. Washington's two important victories kept the struggle for **independence** alive.

■ *General George Washington led his troops across the Delaware River to victory in Trenton. It was an important turning point for the colonial forces. The victory gave Washington's troops the feeling that they could defeat the British.*

General Horatio Gates (left) was born in England. He served in America on the British side during the French and Indian War. When war broke out between the colonies and England, he sided with the colonists.

16

The Battle of Saratoga

The Battle of Saratoga was actually two battles that were fought weeks apart. The British army was in upstate New York, trying to take control of the city of Albany. Their forces were led by General John Burgoyne. On September 19, 1777, the first battle of Saratoga was fought at Freeman's Farm. Though the British were able to hold their position, about 600 British soldiers were killed or hurt.

On October 7, the second battle was fought. The colonists' forces outnumbered the British. General Burgoyne was forced to surrender to American general Horatio Gates. The colonists' success in Saratoga made European countries such as France and Spain see that the colonists had a chance of winning the war against England.

■ *After the Battle of Saratoga, General John Burgoyne (center left, holding sword) surrendered his troops to the colonial forces. After the war, Burgoyne returned to England, where he wrote plays for the theater.*

This French map shows where the Battle of Yorktown took place. Washington's plan to trap the British in Virginia worked so well that it helped lead to the end of the war.

The End of the War

In February 1778, France signed a **treaty** agreeing to join the colonists in their war against England. With France involved, England was forced to protect its other colonies in the West Indies. The British were afraid that these colonies would be attacked by France. On August 1, 1781, British general Charles Cornwallis brought his soldiers to the small port of Yorktown, Virginia, on the Chesapeake Bay. General Washington planned to trap Cornwallis there. A group of French ships sailed from the West Indies, blocking a possible British escape at the Chesapeake Bay. At the same time, Washington's men blocked the British escape by land. Washington's plan worked. The British could not defend themselves against the French and the American colonists. On October 19, 1781, the British surrendered.

■ *General Charles Cornwallis surrendered his troops to colonial forces at Yorktown. He and his men had been surrounded by about 18,000 soldiers and sailors.*

This page (left) is from the Treaty of Paris. The treaty called for England to recognize the independence of the United States.

The New Nation

Several small battles were fought after the Battle of Yorktown. However, England finally agreed to give the colonies their independence. Leaders from America and Great Britain met in France to talk about ending the war. The Treaty of Paris was finalized on September 3, 1783. This treaty recognized the birth of a new nation, the United States of America.

The British kept Canada, but they had to leave the American **territory**. The leaders of the new American nation were now faced with an important job. They had to make a place in the world as a new nation. However, they were finally free to make their own decisions.

■ *The Treaty of Paris was signed by both British and colonial officials. Work began on the treaty in 1782. It was finished in 1783.*

Timeline

1763	England and its North American colonies win the French and Indian War.
1770	Five colonists die fighting British soldiers in Boston. This event is called the Boston Massacre.
1773	Angry colonists dump a shipload of tea into Boston Harbor. This event is called the Boston Tea Party.
1774	The First Continental Congress is formed in Philadelphia, Pennsylvania.
April 19, 1775	The American Revolutionary War begins.
June 1775	The Battle of Bunker Hill is fought. The Continental Army is formed, with George Washingtion as its leader.
July 4, 1776	The Declaration of Independence is approved by the Continental Congress in Philadelphia.
December 26, 1776	George Washington leads about 2,400 troops across the Delaware River. They attack the British forces in Trenton, New Jersey.
October 7, 1777	The Battle of Saratoga is won by the colonists.
February 1778	France joins the war on the side of the colonies.
October 19, 1781	The colonists win the war, earning their freedom from England.
September 3, 1783	The Treaty of Paris is finalized and the United States of America is born.

Glossary

allies (al-EYEZ) People or groups that are joined together for a common cause.

American Revolutionary War (uh-MER-uh-kuhn rev-uh-LOO-shuh-ner-ee WOR) The war from 1775–1783 during which the American colonies fought against England. As a result, the United States of America was created.

Boston Massacre (BAWS-tuhn MASS-uh-kur) A fight between British soldiers and an angry crowd of colonists in Boston, Massachusetts, in 1770.

Continental army (KON-tuh-nuhnt-el AR-mee) The colonial army that fought against the British in the American Revolutionary War.

Continental Congress (KON-tuh-nuhnt-el KON-gress) A group of people picked to decide laws for the American colonies.

Declaration of Independence (dehk-luh-RAY-shuhn UHV in-dih-PEN-duhns) A document declaring the freedom of American colonies from England.

independence (in-di-PEN-duhnss) Being free.

Intolerable Acts (in-TOL-ur-uh-buhl AKTS) A set of strict laws the British passed that angered the colonists and led to their fight for independence.

minutemen (MIN-it-men) Volunteer soldiers in the American Revolutionary War who were ready to fight at a minute's notice.

protest (pruh-TEST) To object to something strongly and publicly.

shipload (SHIP-lohd) As much as a ship will hold.

territory (TER-uh-tor-ee) The land and waters under the control of a state, nation, or ruler.

treaty (TREE-tee) A formal agreement between two or more countries.

weapons (WEP-uhnz) Things that can be used in a fight to attack or defend, such as swords, guns, knives, or bombs.

23

Index

Primary Sources

Cover: *The Death of General Warren at the Battle of Bunker Hill* [1786]. Painting by John Trumbull. Held at Trumbull Collection. Yale University Art Gallery. **Page 4 (inset):** *The General Laws and Liberties of the Massachusets Colony* [1672]. A 1672 printing of the 1648 document. Library of Congress. **Page 4:** Attacking a whale with the hand harpoon [Date Unknown]. Engraving. **Page 6 (inset):** The Stamp Act, 1765 [1766]. Library of Congress. **Page 6:** *The Shooting of General Braddock at Fort Duquesne (Pittsburgh), 1755.* [c. Nineteenth Century]. Oil painting by Edwin Willard Deming. The State Historical Society of Wisconsin, Madison. **Page 8 (inset):** "Boston Tea Party" [1789]. Engraving by W.D. Cooper. Library of Congress. **Page 8:** "The Bloody Massacre Perpetrated in King Street, Boston on March 5, 1770" [1770]. Engraving by Paul Revere. Library of Congress. **Page 10 (inset):** Royal Proclamation [1775]. **Page 10:** "The South Part of Lexington" [1775]. Engraving by Amos Doolittle. Print Collection, Miriam and Ira D. Wallach Division of Art, Prints and Photographs, The New York Public Library, Astor, Lenox and Tilden Foundations. **Page 12 (inset):** Map: Plan of the action which happen'd 17th. June 1775, at Charles Town, N. America. [1775]. Pen and ink and water color by Sir Thomas Hyde Page. Library of Congress. **Page 12:** *Declaration of Independence, 4 July, 1776* [c. 1786-1819]. Painting by John Trumbull. **Page 14 (inset):** "L 'Entré triumphale of troupes royals a Nouvelle Yorck" [c. 1770s]. Hand-colored engraving. Library of Congress. **Page 14:** *Washington Crossing the Delaware* [1851]. Painting by Emmanuel Gottlieb Leutze. Metropolitan Museum of Art. **Page 16:** *Horatio Gates* [1782]. Painting by Charles Willson Peale. Independence National Historic Park. **Page 16:** *Surrender of General Burgoyne at Saratoga* [c. 1791]. Painting by John Trumbull. Architect of the Capitol. **Page 18 (inset):** Map of the Battle of Yorktown [1781]. Created by Esnaunts et Rapilly. Paris, France. Publisher copy held at Maryland State Archives. **Page 18:** *Surrender of Cornwallis at Yorktown* [1817]. Painting by John Trumbull. Architect of the Capitol. **Page 20(inset):** The Treaty of Paris [1783]. National Archives. **Page 20:** Signing the preliminary treaty of peace at Paris, November 30, 1782 [Date Unknown]. Painting C. Seiler. Library of Congress.

Web Sites

Due to the changing nature of Internet links, PowerKids Press has developed an online list of Web sites related to the topic of this book. This site is updated regularly. Please use this link to access the list:
http://www.powerkidslinks.com/psaw/arw/